THE GOSPEL OF JESUS CHRIST

PAUL WASHER

REFORMATION HERITAGE BOOKS
GRAND RAPIDS, MICHIGAN

The Gospel of Jesus Christ
© 2016 by Paul Washer

Reformation Heritage Books
3070 29th St. SE
Grand Rapids, MI 49512
616-977-0889
orders@heritagebooks.org
www.heritagebooks.org

Printed in the United States of America
21 22 23 24 25 26/14 13 12 11 10 9 8

Scripture taken from the New King James Version®. Copyright © 1982 by Thomas Nelson. Used by permission. All rights reserved.

ISBN 978-1-60178-520-6

ISBN 978-1-60178-521-3 (epub)

For additional Reformed literature, request a free book list from Reformation Heritage Books at the above regular or e-mail address.

CONTENTS

THE GOSPEL OF JESUS CHRIST

The central message of Christianity is the gospel of Jesus Christ. The word *gospel* means "good news." Christianity offers the best news of all time! Indeed, it offers the only solution to our most pressing crises. No educational program, political party, or psychological therapy is able to address the deepest problem of the human race. Though human wisdom has brought many temporary benefits to us, history has also revealed how bankrupt we are to address the profound guilt and pervasive corruption under which our world groans.

The gospel reveals that God has come and won the victory for us. It is good news precisely because it is not about what we have done or can do, but what God has done and will do on behalf of His people. The gospel declares divine intervention into a hopeless world.

The gospel announces the good news of the coming of Jesus Christ. Approximately two thousand years ago, during the height of the Roman Empire, God sent His Son into human history in order to save people of every nation from their sins and misery. Christ was conceived by the Spirit of God in the womb of a virgin and was born Jesus of Nazareth, the God-man.

Jesus came to bear the sins of fallen men and women and to offer His life as a sacrifice in our place. His death satisfied the demands of God's justice against sinners and made it possible for a just God to pardon them. His resurrection three days later testified that He is the Son of God and that God accepted His death as full payment for our sin. Now, all people may be fully forgiven, reconciled to God, and receive eternal life through faith in the person and work of Jesus Christ. Through this great work of salvation, God has revealed to us who He is.

THE CHARACTER OF GOD

To understand the gospel, we must understand something about God. God is not an impersonal force or energy all around us, but the personal

---

I wish to thank Paul M. Smalley for his helpful editing assistance on this booklet.

Creator and Lord of all (Genesis 1). The Bible teaches us that the only true God exists as a Trinity: Father, Son, and Holy Spirit (Matthew 3:16–17; 28:19). They are three distinct persons who are distinguishable from one another, and yet they are one being, not three (John 10:30–33). They share the one divine essence with the same divine qualities. Because of these qualities, which make God uniquely Himself, the Lord requires a sacrifice for sin if sinners are to be saved. To see the need for Christ's death, therefore, we must know more about the character of this triune God.

GOD IS LOVE

The Bible teaches us that God is love (1 John 4:8) and that His love moves Him to freely and selflessly give Himself to others for their benefit or good. It is important to understand that God's love is much more than an attitude, an emotion, or something that He does. Instead, love is an attribute of God—His very being or nature. God not only loves; He *is* love. He is the essence of what love is, and all true love flows from Him as its ultimate source. Other words that are often associated with the love of God are benevolence, mercy, grace, and patience. Regardless of what we may think or even hear, the unwavering testimony of the Bible is that God is love!

He who does not love does not know God, for God is love. (1 John 4:8)

The Lord is merciful and gracious, slow to anger, and abounding in mercy. (Psalm 103:8; see also Exodus 34:6; Psalms 86:15; 145:8)

Therefore the Lord will wait, that He may be gracious to you; and therefore He will be exalted, that He may have mercy on you. (Isaiah 30:18)

Every good gift and every perfect gift is from above, and comes down from the Father of lights, with whom there is no variation or shadow of turning. (James 1:17)

GOD IS HOLY

The Bible teaches us that God is holy (Isaiah 6:3). The word communicates the idea of being "separated," "marked off," or "placed apart." With regard to God, it has two important meanings. First, it means that God is above all His creation and is totally distinct from every created being. Regardless of their splendor, all other beings on earth and in heaven are mere creatures. God alone is God—separate, transcendent, and incomparable. Second, the holiness of God means that He is above, or separated from, the moral corruption of His creation and from all that is profane and sinful. God cannot sin, cannot take pleasure in sin, and cannot have fellowship with sin.

> And one cried to another and said:
> "Holy, holy, holy is the Lord of hosts;
> The whole earth is full of His glory!" (Isaiah 6:3)

God is light and in Him is no darkness at all. (1 John 1:5)

You are of purer eyes than to behold evil, and cannot look on wickedness. (Habbakuk 1:13)

Let no one say when he is tempted, "I am tempted by God"; for God cannot be tempted by evil, nor does He Himself tempt anyone. (James 1:13)

For You are not a God who takes pleasure in wickedness, nor shall evil dwell with You. (Psalm 5:4)

GOD IS RIGHTEOUS

The word *righteous* tells us of the moral excellence of God. According to the Bible, God is an absolutely righteous being and always acts in a way that is perfectly consistent with who He is. There is nothing wrong or incorrect about God's nature or His works. He will never be or do anything that would justify any accusation of wrongdoing against Him. His works, decrees, and judgments are absolutely perfect.

> For the LORD is righteous,
> He loves righteousness;
> His countenance beholds the upright. (Psalm 11:7)

He is the Rock, His work is perfect;
For all His ways are justice,
A God of truth and without injustice;
Righteous and upright is He. (Deuteronomy 32:4)

The righteousness of God not only describes His character but also His relationship to His creation, especially to humanity. According to the Bible, God has revealed His will to all people through His creation (Romans 1:20, 32) and through their consciences (Romans 2:14–16). He has most clearly revealed Himself by His Word, the Bible (Psalm 19:7–11). He will judge every person according to the standard that has been revealed to them. There will come a day in which God will judge everyone according to the strictest standards of justice and fairness, rewarding the good that is done and punishing the evil.

But the LORD shall endure forever;
He has prepared His throne for judgment.
He shall judge the world in righteousness,
And He shall administer judgment for the peoples in
    uprightness. (Psalm 9:7–8)

For God will bring every work into judgment,
Including every secret thing,
Whether good or evil. (Ecclesiastes 12:14; see also
    Proverbs 5:21; 15:3; Hebrews 4:13)

I, the LORD, search the heart,
I test the mind,
Even to give every man according to his ways,
According to the fruit of his doings. (Jeremiah 17:10;
    see also Hebrews 9:27)

We must always recognize that God's judgment of man is not unwarranted or cruel, but is a consequence of His righteous character and a necessary part of His government. A God who would refuse to judge wickedness would not be loving, good, or righteous. A creation where wickedness was not restrained and judged would soon self-destruct.

Have you met this God? It is one thing to talk about God, but quite another to encounter His glory in the Bible. Where God is truly known, all mankind becomes as nothing. The least glimpse of His holiness humbles us and threatens to undo us. Even in our original, pristine condition when God first made us, we were mere images and servants, and He was almighty God. Yet we have fallen far lower because of our sin against Him.

THE CHARACTER OF HUMANITY

To grasp and appreciate the gospel, we must not only understand something about the character of God but also something about our character. What the Bible has to say about us is not flattering or pleasant, but it is accurate.

HUMANITY IS MORALLY CORRUPT

Before he fell into sin, man's original state was noble, but man's present condition is desperate. The Bible teaches us that although humankind was created good (Genesis 1:26, 31), all humans have fallen into spiritual death (Ephesians 2:1). We are by nature morally corrupt, inclined toward evil, and hostile toward the righteous God.

> Truly, this only I have found:
> That God made man upright,
> But they have sought out many schemes. (Ecclesiastes 7:29)

> The heart is deceitful above all things,
> And desperately wicked;
> Who can know it? (Jeremiah 17:9)

> For out of the heart proceed evil thoughts, murders, adulteries, fornications, thefts, false witness, blasphemies. (Matthew 15:19)

> But we are all like an unclean thing,
> And all our righteousnesses are like filthy rags;
> We all fade as a leaf,
> And our iniquities, like the wind,
> Have taken us away. (Isaiah 64:6)

Because the carnal mind is enmity [hatred] against God; for it is not subject to the law of God, neither indeed can be. (Romans 8:7)

The Bible verses that you have just read may offend you; their indictment of humanity, however, is attested on every page of history. Furthermore, if you are honest with yourself, you will admit that the truth of these verses is also confirmed by your thoughts, words, and deeds, which continually break the holy law of God's Ten Commandments (Exodus 20:1–17; see Matthew 5:21–48).

GUILTY AND CONDEMNED

The Bible teaches us that our inward moral corruption leads us to commit acts against the righteous standard of a holy, just, and loving God. All of us, without exception, are sinners both by nature and by the deeds that we have committed. All of us stand guilty and without excuse before God.

For all have sinned and fall short of the glory of God.
  (Romans 3:23)

There is no one who does not sin. (1 Kings 8:46)

As it is written:
    "There is none righteous, no, not one;
    There is none who understands;
    There is none who seeks after God.
    They have all turned aside;
    They have together become unprofitable;
    There is none who does good, no, not one."
      (Romans 3:10–12)

Now we know that whatever the law says, it says to those who are under the law, that every mouth may be stopped, and all the world may become guilty before God. (Romans 3:19)

If You, LORD, should mark iniquities, O Lord, who could stand? (Psalm 130:3)

Examine yourself. Are you a sinner? This is not a question of whether you make some mistakes. Nor is it a matter of simply acknowledging that you have done a few wrong things. Do you recognize that you have a sinful heart and a record of breaking God's laws? Don't make excuses. Don't pretend that you are a basically good person. If you do, then Jesus has nothing for you, for He came for sinners. However, if you acknowledge your sin with grief, then God's wisdom has solved your great problem in the most remarkable way.

THE GREAT DILEMMA

It is comforting to know that God is holy and righteous. It would be ter-rifying if the omnipotent Ruler of the universe were evil. To the thinking man, however, the absolute goodness of God is also disturbing. If God is good, what will He do with those of us who are not? What will a good and righteous God do with human beings who are self-centered, inclined to evil, and disobedient? If the Judge of all the earth deals with us on the basis of justice, shouldn't He condemn us all?

These questions lead us to the greatest of all religious and philo-sophical dilemmas: How can God be just, yet pardon those who should justly be condemned? How can God be holy, yet befriend those who are evil? Anyone who justifies the wicked is an abomination to the Lord (Proverbs 17:15). How then can the Lord justify sinners like us and still be just (Romans 3:26)?

GOD'S ANSWER TO OUR DILEMMA

If God acts according to His justice, then the sinner must be condemned. If God pardons the sinner, then His justice is compromised. The answer to this greatest of all dilemmas can be found only in the gospel. In jus-tice, God condemned humanity and demanded complete satisfaction for our crimes against Him. In love, God took humanity upon Himself, bore our sin, suffered the penalty we deserved, and died in our place. The same God whose justice demanded satisfaction for our sin made satis-faction by offering Himself in our place. This is what makes the gospel truly good news!

JESUS CHRIST, OUR SUBSTITUTE

According to the Bible, the Father's love for us moved Him to give His Son as a sacrifice for our sins, and the Son's love for us moved Him to offer Himself willingly for us.

For God so loved the world that He gave His only begotten Son, that whoever believes in Him should not perish but have everlasting life. (John 3:16)

God is love. In this the love of God was manifested toward us, that God has sent His only begotten Son into the world, that we might live through Him. In this is love, not that we loved God, but that He loved us and sent His Son to be the propitiation for our sins. (1 John 4:8–10)

[Jesus said,] "Greater love has no one than this, than to lay down one's life for his friends." (John 15:13)

THE CROSS

Upon the cross, Jesus Christ, the Son of God, offered Himself as a sacrifice for His people's sin. Most historians consider the cross to be the cruelest mechanism of torture that mankind has ever devised. This cruelty serves to illustrate two important realities.

First, this cruelty illustrates the greatness of our hostility toward God. God so loved the world that He gave His only Son, and the world so hated God that it subjected Him to the worst form of torture and death.

Second, it illustrates the greatness of our sin against God. Our crimes against God were so deplorable and the penalties against us so severe that they could be paid for only through the indescribable suffering and death of the Son of God!

The physical suffering and death that Christ endured on the cross were absolutely necessary. We must understand, however, that His suffering involved more than just the cruelty of evil men. On the cross Christ suffered the judgment of God! God's justice demanded satisfaction for our sins, and His wrath was kindled against us. To satisfy God's justice and appease His wrath, it was necessary that Christ suffer the judgment we deserved. Thus, He bore our sin, became a curse in our place, was abandoned by God, and suffered the full measure of God's wrath against us.

Christ Bore Our Sin. On the cross, our sins were imputed to Christ. That means God placed our sins on Christ's account and considered them

His. Consequently, Christ was declared guilty before the judgment throne of God and was treated as the guilty party.

> All we like sheep have gone astray;
> We have turned, every one, to his own way;
> And the LORD has laid on Him the iniquity of us all. (Isaiah 53:6)

> For [God] has made [Christ] who knew no sin to be sin for us, that we might become the righteousness of God in Him. (2 Corinthians 5:21)

Christ Suffered Our Curse. To be cursed of God is to become an object of His displeasure and condemnation. All of us were under God's curse because of our sin. To save us from the curse, Christ became a curse for us and suffered the judgment of God in our place. He redeemed us, which means that He paid the price to satisfy divine justice in order that all who believe in Him are set free.

> For as many as are of the works of the law are under the curse; for it is written, "Cursed is everyone who does not continue in all things which are written in the book of the law, to do them." (Galatians 3:10)

> Christ has redeemed us from the curse of the law, having become a curse for us (for it is written, "Cursed is everyone who hangs on a tree"). (Galatians 3:13)

Christ Was Forsaken by God in Our Place. One of the most terrifying results of our sin is alienation from God—to be shut out of His favorable presence and communion.

> But your iniquities have separated you from your God;
> And your sins have hidden His face from you,
> So that He will not hear. (Isaiah 59:2)

To save us from such eternal separation, Christ bore our sins on Calvary and was forsaken by God in our place.

And about the ninth hour Jesus cried out with a loud voice, saying, "Eli, Eli, lama sabachthani?" that is, "My God, My God, why
have You forsaken Me?" (Matthew 27:46)

Christ Suffered the Wrath of God for Us. The Bible teaches us that God
is angry with man because of his unrelenting evil, although this is an
unpopular truth. Psalm 7:11 declares, "God is a just judge, and God is
angry with the wicked every day."

God's anger is not an uncontrollable, irrational, or selfish emotion
but a result of His holiness, righteousness, and love for all that is good.
God hates sin and comes with terrible and often violent wrath against it.
If man is an object of God's wrath, it is because he has chosen to chal-
lenge God's sovereignty, violate His will, and give himself to evil.

Since all men are guilty of sin, they deserve God's wrath. In love,
however, Christ took the cup of God's wrath that we deserve and drank
down every drop until it was completely depleted and the justice of God
against us was fully satisfied.

> For thus says the Lord God of Israel to me: "Take this wine cup
> of fury from My hand, and cause all the nations, to whom I send
> you, to drink it." (Jeremiah 25:15)

> He went a little farther and fell on His face, and prayed, saying,
> "O My Father, if it is possible, let this cup pass from Me; never-
> theless, not as I will, but as You will…. Again, a second time, He
> went away and prayed, saying, "O My Father, if this cup cannot
> pass away from Me unless I drink it, Your will be done." (Mat-
> thew 26:39, 42)

> Surely He has borne our griefs
> And carried our sorrows;
> Yet we esteemed Him stricken,
> Smitten by God, and afflicted.
> But He was wounded for our transgressions,
> He was bruised for our iniquities; the chastisement for our
>   peace was upon Him,
> And by His stripes we are healed. (Isaiah 53:4–5)

Christ Died in Our Place. One of the greatest proofs of the judgment of God against our unrighteousness is physical death—the separation of the soul from the body. From the time of Adam until the present, all people are faced with the terrible and undeniable reality that they will die (Romans 5:12). The Bible teaches us that death was not an original or natural part of creation. Instead, it is a judgment of God upon people because of their sin. In order to save us from the power of death, it was necessary that Christ die in our place.

> For the wages of sin is death. (Romans 6:23)

> And when Jesus had cried out with a loud voice, He said, "Father, 'into Your hands I commit My spirit.'" Having said this, He breathed His last. (Luke 23:46)

> For Christ also suffered once for sins, the just for the unjust, that He might bring us to God, being put to death in the flesh but made alive by the Spirit. (1 Peter 3:18)

Christ did not die as a mere martyr, but as the Redeemer of sinful humanity. Before He breathed His last breath, He declared, "It is finished!" (John 19:30). When He said this, He meant that through His suffering and death, He made full payment for the sins of those who believe in Him.

Do you believe that Christ died for sinners? If you do not, then why are you resisting the word of the God who cannot lie? If you do believe it, then how has this great truth affected you? Do you remain indifferent to the crucified Lord? Or worse, do you use the cross of Christ as an excuse to live a wicked, immoral life? If Christ's death has truly come home to your heart, then you will no longer be able to live for yourself but will be inwardly compelled to live for the One who died and rose again for you. Once God opens your eyes to see His wisdom and power in the cross, you will never be the same again but will follow the risen Christ.

THE RESURRECTION

It is the testimony of the Bible that Christ not only died for the sins of His people but that He was raised from the dead on the third day. The resurrection of Jesus Christ is foundational to Christianity. If Christ was not raised, then the gospel is a myth and our faith is useless (1 Corinthians 15:14). But since Christ's resurrection is a historical fact, it validates everything that He both claimed to be and to do on our behalf.

The Resurrection Is Proof That Jesus Is the Son of God. In John 2:18–19, the leaders of the Jews asked Jesus for a sign to show that He had the authority to cleanse God's temple. In response, Jesus answered, "Destroy this temple, and in three days I will raise it up." In Romans 1:4, the apostle Paul wrote that Jesus was "declared to be the Son of God with power according to the Spirit of holiness, by the resurrection from the dead." This does not mean that Jesus became the Son at the resurrection, but that the resurrection was the Father's validation that Jesus was the eternal Son of God.

The Resurrection Is Proof That God Accepted Christ's Death as Full Payment for Our Sin. Romans 4:25 says that Christ "was delivered up because of our offenses, and was raised because of our justification." The meaning of the text is that God raised Jesus Christ because His death had satisfied God's justice and secured the believer's pardon and right standing before God (justification).

The Resurrection Is Proof of the Believer's Future Resurrection. In John 11:25 Jesus declared, "I am the resurrection and the life. He who believes in Me, though he may die, he shall live." This promise would have proven null and void if Christ had remained in the tomb. His authority over death was demonstrated in His own resurrection. It proves that He has the power to raise to life all who believe in Him. In 1 Corinthians 6:14, the apostle Paul wrote, "God both raised up the Lord and will also raise us up by His power."

The Resurrection Is Proof That the World Has a Lord and a Judge. The Bible teaches us that Christ was not only raised to life but that God exalted Him to be Lord and Judge over all creation. In the first sermon preached after the resurrection, the apostle Peter declared to the Jews, "Therefore let all the house of Israel know assuredly that God has made this Jesus, whom you crucified, both Lord and Christ" (Acts 2:36). The apostle Paul also declared this truth:

> Therefore God also has highly exalted Him and given Him the name which is above every name, that at the name of Jesus every knee should bow, of those in heaven, and of those on earth, and of those under the earth. (Philippians 2:9–10)

> God…commands all men everywhere to repent, because He has appointed a day on which He will judge the world in righteousness by the Man whom He has ordained. He has given assurance of this to all by raising Him from the dead. (Acts 17:30–31)

The good news of the resurrection shows us that Christianity is not just a list of rules or a philosophy of life. It is not merely something to debate or hold a position on. At the heart of Christianity is the living person of Jesus Christ. The Lord Jesus speaks through His Word, the Bible, today and powerfully saves sinners. Have you met Him? Has He saved you by the glorious accomplishment of His death and resurrection?

CHRIST'S ACCOMPLISHMENT

Immediately before His death, Christ declared, "It is finished!" (John 19:30). This brief statement was Christ's declaration of victory. By His death He accomplished all that was necessary for humanity's salvation. The demands of God's justice against us were satisfied, and His wrath was appeased. God is both just and the justifier of wicked people (Romans 3:26). On the cross of Christ, "mercy and truth have met together; righteousness and peace have kissed" (Psalm 85:10). Now, pardon and justification are available to all through faith in the person and work of Christ.

> Therefore, having been justified by faith, we have peace with God through our Lord Jesus Christ…. There is therefore now no condemnation to those who are in Christ Jesus, who do not walk according to the flesh, but according to the Spirit. (Romans 5:1; 8:1)

Jesus said to him, "I am the way, the truth, and the life. No one comes to the Father except through Me." (John 14:6)

Nor is there salvation in any other, for there is no other name under heaven given among men by which we must be saved. (Acts 4:12)

For there is one God and one Mediator between God and men, the Man Christ Jesus. (1 Timothy 2:5)

OUR RESPONSE

Having considered God's work on behalf of sinful humanity, we must now ask how we are to respond in order to benefit from such a great salvation, or, what must we do to be saved? The Bible demands two things of all men: (1) that they repent of their sins, and (2) that they trust in the person and work of Jesus Christ:

[Jesus Christ said], "The time is fulfilled, and the kingdom of God is at hand. Repent, and believe in the gospel." (Mark 1:15)

[The apostle Paul was] "testifying to Jews, and also to Greeks, repentance toward God and faith toward our Lord Jesus Christ. (Acts 20:21)

REPENTANCE

Repentance is a gift of God (Acts 11:18) and a work of the Holy Spirit in the sinner's heart that results in a change of mind (1 Thessalonians 1:5, 9). This may seem superficial until we understand that the heart refers to the control center of our intellect, will, and emotions. For this reason, a change of mind will always be proven genuine by real changes in our attitudes and conduct.

A wonderful example of repentance is found in the life of Saul of Tarsus, later to be known as the apostle Paul. In his ignorance and unbelief, he thought that Jesus of Nazareth was nothing more than an impostor and a blasphemer and that all who followed Him were the enemies of God and worthy of death (Acts 9:1–2; 1 Timothy 1:13). On his way to Damascus, however, Saul was confronted by the resurrected

Christ (Acts 9:3–8) and discovered that he had been wrong about Him. He had thought that Jesus was a blasphemer, only to discover that He was the Son of God, the promised Messiah, and the Savior of the world. He had thought that righteousness was earned through obedience to the law, only to discover that there was nothing good in him (Romans 7:18) and that salvation was a gift of God (Ephesians 2:8–9). He had thought that the disciples of Jesus were the enemies of Israel and unfit to live (Acts 8:1), only to discover that he was persecuting the true Israel (Galatians 6:16) and putting to death the sons and daughters of the living God (Romans 8:14–15).

Through one encounter with Christ Jesus, Saul of Tarsus, the proud and self-righteous Pharisee of Pharisees, was proven wrong. He repented and immediately began to proclaim Jesus in the synagogues, saying, "He is the Son of God" (Acts 9:18–22). The news spread throughout all the churches of Judea that "He who formerly persecuted us now preaches the faith which he once tried to destroy" (Galatians 1:22–23). Paul's change of mind led to a change in everything else!

Changes in Our Thinking. Repentance involves a change of mind leading to a recognition that what God says is true and that we have been wrong.

> For I acknowledge my transgressions,
> And my sin is always before me.
> Against You, You only, have I sinned,
> And done this evil in Your sight—
> That You may be found just when You speak,
> And blameless when You judge. (Psalm 51:3–4)

> And I prayed to the LORD my God, and made confession, and said, "O Lord, great and awesome God, who keeps His covenant and mercy with those who love Him, and with those who keep His commandments, we have sinned and committed iniquity, we have done wickedly and rebelled, even by departing from Your precepts and Your judgments." (Daniel 9:4–5)

Changes in Our Emotions. A genuine recognition of our sinfulness and guilt will also lead to genuine sorrow, shame, and even hatred for what we have become and done. We begin to disdain, with a deep sense of shame and remorse, the sin we once loved.

> And there you shall remember your ways and all your doings with which you were defiled; and you shall loathe yourselves in your own sight because of all the evils that you have committed. (Ezekiel 20:43)

> Surely, after my turning, I repented;
> And after I was instructed, I struck myself on the thigh;
> I was ashamed, yes, even humiliated,
> Because I bore the reproach of my youth. (Jeremiah 31:19)

> For what I am doing, I do not understand. For what I will to do, that I do not practice; but what I hate, that I do.... O wretched man that I am! Who will deliver me from this body of death? (Romans 7:15, 24)

> Now I rejoice, not that you were made sorry, but that your sorrow led to repentance. For you were made sorry in a godly manner, that you might suffer loss from us in nothing. (2 Corinthians 7:9)

> The sacrifices of God are a broken spirit,
> A broken and a contrite heart—
> These, O God, You will not despise. (Psalm 51:17)

Changes in Our Actions. Our claim to think differently and our expressed emotions against sin are not in themselves definite evidence of genuine repentance. True repentance will also be accompanied by a change of the will that produces right actions—especially, a turning away from sin and a turning to God in obedience.

> Therefore bear fruits worthy of repentance. (Matthew 3:8)

> They should repent, turn to God, and do works befitting repentance. (Acts 26:20)

For they themselves declare concerning us what manner of entry we had to you, and how you turned to God from idols to serve the living and true God, and to wait for His Son from heaven, whom He raised from the dead, even Jesus who delivers us from the wrath to come. (1 Thessalonians 1:9–10)

SELF-EXAMINATION: ARE YOU REPENTING?

We have learned that we must repent to be saved. The question that now remains to be answered is personal: Have you repented? Are you repenting? The following exploratory questions will help you determine if genuine repentance is a reality in your life.

1. Do you now think differently about God? Do you see that God, rather than you, should be at the center of all things? Do you lament your neglect of God? Are you beginning to recognize His worth? Do you desire to seek Him and know Him?

2. Do you now think differently about sin? Do you see that sin is vile and a terrible offense to God? Do you feel regret and shame for your sin? Do you long to be free from both the condemnation and the slavery of sin? Are you determined to confess your sin and turn to God for mercy?

3. Do you now think differently about the way of salvation? Do you fully agree that you cannot return to God by your own merit, but only through the person and work of Christ? Do you acknowledge that your best deeds are like filthy rags before God, and have you rejected all hope in your own righteousness?

If you are able to affirm these questions, and if these things are growing realities in your life, it is an indication that God has been and is working in your heart, illuminating your mind to see the truth and granting you repentance unto salvation.

If you are unable to affirm these questions but desire salvation, then continue to seek God in His Word and in prayer. Reconsider the Bible verses that we have studied and examine your life in light of them.

Continue to cry out to God, and seek Him in His Word until He has wrought a change in your heart.

FAITH

With repentance unto life comes saving faith. Faith is more than a belief in the existence of God; it also involves a trust, confidence, or reliance upon His character and the truthfulness of His word. The Bible declares, "You believe that there is one God. You do well. Even the demons believe—and tremble!" (James 2:19). People with genuine faith do not merely believe there is a God but they trust what He has said and rely upon it.

Faith Defined. The Bible defines faith as "the substance of things hoped for, the evidence of things not seen" (Hebrews 11:1). This leads us to a very important question: How can a reasonable person be assured of what he or she hopes for or have the conviction that what he or she has never seen actually exists?

The answer to this question is found in the character of God, the trustworthiness of the Bible, and the ministry of the Holy Spirit. We can be assured of forgiveness of sin, reconciliation with God, and the hope of eternal life because God has promised these things in the Bible (Titus 1:2–3), and the Spirit of God testifies to our hearts that they are true (John 16:13; Romans 8:14–16; Galatians 4:6; 1 John 2:20, 27).

Faith Focused. Saving faith especially consists of trust that Christ is our Savior, our only righteousness with God. One of the greatest evidences of genuine repentance is that we are not only turning away from sin but we are also turning away from trusting in our own virtue, merits, or works to gain a right standing before God. We realize that all our supposed personal righteousness and good deeds are as filthy rags (Isaiah 64:6), and we firmly reject them as a means of salvation. We know that if we are to be reconciled to God, it will not be as a result of our works for Him but as a result of His great work for us through Jesus Christ. We agree unreservedly with the following Bible verses.

> Knowing that a man is not justified by the works of the law but by faith in Jesus Christ, even we have believed in Christ Jesus, that we might be justified by faith in Christ and not by the works

of the law; for by the works of the law no flesh shall be justified. (Galatians 2:16)

Now to him who works, the wages are not counted as grace but as debt. But to him who does not work but believes on Him who justifies the ungodly, his faith is accounted for righteousness. (Romans 4:4–5)

For by grace you have been saved through faith, and that not of yourselves; it is the gift of God, not of works, lest anyone should boast. (Ephesians 2:8–9)

Faith Illustrated. In the life of Abraham, the Bible provides us with a wonderful illustration of genuine faith. When Abraham and his wife, Sarah, were far beyond the age of having children, God promised them a son. In response to this promise, the Bible declares that Abraham was "fully convinced that what He had promised He was also able to perform" (Romans 4:21). Abraham believed God, and it was credited to him as righteousness (Romans 4:3).

With regard to the gospel, genuine faith involves believing in and relying upon what God has revealed about Himself, about us, and about His work of salvation through the life, death, and resurrection of Jesus Christ. To believe is to be fully assured that what God has promised through Jesus Christ, He is really willing and able to perform. The following Bible verses are a good representation of what God has promised.

For God so loved the world that He gave His only begotten Son, that whoever believes in Him should not perish but have everlasting life. (John 3:16)

But as many as received Him, to them He gave the right to become children of God, to those who believe in His name. (John 1:12)

[Jesus said,] "Most assuredly, I say to you, he who hears My word and believes in Him who sent Me has everlasting life, and shall not come into judgment, but has passed from death into life." (John 5:24)

SELF-EXAMINATION: ARE YOU BELIEVING?

We must believe in Jesus Christ to be saved. The question that now remains to be answered is personal: Have you believed? Are you believing, trusting, and relying upon the person and work of Jesus Christ? The following exploratory questions will help you determine if genuine faith is a reality in your life.

1. Are you convinced that salvation is found in no other name except Jesus Christ? Are you convinced that the claims of all other so-called prophets and saviors are false? Do you trust your eternal well-being to the power and faithfulness of just one person—Jesus of Nazareth?

2. Are you convinced that salvation is not a result of your own virtue or merit? Are you convinced that even your most righteous deeds are like filthy rags before God? Are you convinced that salvation by works is utterly hopeless?

3. Have you rested your full trust in the Son of God to save you from your sins? Are you depending upon Him to teach you the truth from the Bible, to forgive your sins by His blood, and to change your heart by His Spirit?

If you are able to affirm these questions, it is an indication that God has been and is working in your heart, illuminating your mind to see the truth, and that you believe unto salvation.

If you are unable to affirm these questions but desire salvation, then continue to seek God in His Word (the Bible) and through prayer. Reconsider the promises that we have studied and examine your life in light of them. Continue to cry out to God to overcome your unbelief and to save you. The Bible promises, "Whoever calls on the name of the LORD shall be saved" (Romans 10:13). Continue to seek Him in His Word until the Spirit of God gives you assurance that you are a child of God.

The Spirit Himself bears witness with our spirit that we are children of God. (Romans 8:16)

And because you are sons, God has sent forth the Spirit of His Son into your hearts, crying out, "Abba, Father!" (Galatians 4:6)

THE ASSURANCE OF SALVATION

Jesus warned that not everyone who claims to be a Christian or even confesses Him as Lord will enter into the kingdom of heaven (Matthew 7:21). On the day of judgment, many will be horrified to learn that they were deceived and that Christ never knew them (Matthew 7:23). This unsettling fact leads us to a very important question: How can we know that we have truly believed and that we have eternal life?

True disciples of Jesus Christ are known by their fruits (Matthew 7:16, 19). In other words, there are observable evidences of genuine faith. Salvation is *not* a result of works, but works are evidence of salvation. James writes, "Show me your faith without your works, and I will show you my faith by my works.... Faith without works is dead" (James 2:18, 26).

Salvation is the result of a supernatural, recreating work of God in the heart by the Holy Spirit. For this reason, the apostle Paul writes, "Therefore, if anyone is in Christ, he is a new creation; old things have passed away; behold, all things have become new" (2 Corinthians 5:17). If we have truly believed in Christ, then we really are new creatures, with new desires that cause us to want to know God and please Him. Because of this, we will begin to live a life that increasingly reflects God's work of salvation in us.

This does not mean that salvation is by faith and works or that we must keep ourselves saved by what we do. It simply means that the new birth (John 3:3, 5) and the continuing work of God in our lives (Ephesians 2:10; Philippians 1:6; 2:13) will ensure that we will reflect the evidences of being a child of God. As Christians, we will have great struggles with sin, and we may even fall into grievous sin for a time. If we are truly born again, however, we will not be able to remain in such a condition, but we will repent and continue to grow in conformity to Christ. This is assured because the God who began a good work in us will complete it (Philippians 1:6).

EVIDENCES OF CONVERSION

The Bible teaches us that Christians should examine, or test, themselves to see if they are in the faith (2 Corinthians 13:5). For such an examination to be accurate, however, we must have a true standard. It is not wise to judge ourselves according to our own or others' opinions. The Word of God is the only proper standard for judging the genuineness of our faith in order to grow in the assurance of our salvation. There is one book in the Bible written specifically for this very purpose—1 John. John writes, "These things I have written to you who believe in the name of the Son of God, that you may know that you have eternal life, and that you may continue to believe in the name of the Son of God" (1 John 5:13).

First John sets forth several characteristics that will be found to some degree in the life of every true Christian. To the degree that these characteristics are evident in our own lives, we may have assurance that we have truly come to know Christ and are being transformed by His power. These marks of genuine conversion are summarized in the following statements. We would do well to carefully and prayerfully examine ourselves in light of them.

1. Christians walk in the light (1 John 1:5–7). Christians' character and conduct are progressively and gradually being conformed to the will of God as He has revealed it to us in the Bible.

2. Christians are sensitive to the sin that is in their life and confess it (1 John 1:8–10). Christians are not immune to sin, but they disdain it and struggle against it. Their lives are marked by repentance, confession, and gradual victory.

3. Christians keep the commandments of God (1 John 2:3–4). Christians practice righteousness (1 John 2:29; 3:7, 10) and do not give themselves to sin as a style of life (1 John 3:4, 6, 8–9). Christians' lives are marked by conformity to the will of God and confession and repentance of departures from God's standard. This does not mean that Christians are capable of perfect obedience to God's commands. It means that the way they live will reflect a new and increasing

appreciation for the commandments of God and a growing conformity or obedience to them.

4. Christians seek to walk as Jesus walked (1 John 2:6). The great ambition of true disciples is to be like their Master (Matthew 10:25). They desire to imitate Christ in everything (1 Corinthians 11:1; Ephesians 5:1). Consequently, Christians also have a growing disinterest in imitating this fallen world or winning its approval.

5. Christians love other Christians, desire their fellowship, and serve them in practical works (1 John 2:9–11). This is one of the greatest evidences of salvation (Matthew 25:34–40; 1 John 3:14–18).

6. Christians grow in their disdain for and rejection of the world (1 John 2:15–17). "The world" refers to the ideas, attitudes, and deeds of this present fallen age that contradict and oppose the nature and will of God.

7. Christians continue in the teachings and practices of the faith that were once and for all handed down to the church through Christ and His apostles (1 John 2:19, 24; Jude 3). Christians have been taught by God (Jeremiah 31:34; John 6:45) and are not carried away by every wind of false doctrine (Ephesians 4:14).

8. Christians purify themselves (1 John 3:3). They seek to grow in holiness, which is moral purity (2 Corinthians 7:1; 1 Timothy 4:7; 1 Peter 1:15–16). This involves not only a separation from evil but also a drawing near to God and a holding on to what is good.

9. Christians believe and confess that Jesus is the Christ, the Son of God and the Savior of the world (1 John 2:22–23; 4:2, 13–15). Christians' great and only hope of salvation is in the person and work of Christ. They believe the testimony of eternal life that God has given them through His Son, Jesus Christ (1 John 5:10–12).

10. Christians are subject to God's loving and paternal discipline (Hebrews 12:5–11). God will not allow His children to continue in immaturity and disobedience, but will discipline them in order that they might share in His holiness and bear the fruit of righteousness. This is one of the great marks or characteristics of true conversion.

THE BENEFITS OF SALVATION

Although we cannot properly set forth and describe all the benefits of salvation in a booklet, it is helpful for us to review a few of them. First, the Christian is regenerated. The Bible teaches us that all people are born spiritually dead and unwilling to respond to God in love and obedience (Romans 8:7; Ephesians 2:1). Those who believe in Christ, however, have been regenerated (Titus 3:5), or made spiritually alive (Ephesians 2:5), so that they might walk in newness of life (Romans 6:4). The believer is a new creation with a new heart that delights in God and desires to please Him (Ezekiel 36:26–27; 2 Corinthians 5:17; 1 John 5:3). This is the true meaning of the phrase "born again" (John 3:3; see also John 3:5; 1 John 5:1). We have not just changed our minds—God has changed our very natures!

Second, the Christian is justified before God (Romans 5:1). This means that not only are we forgiven of all our past, present, and future sins but also that the perfectly righteous life of Christ is imputed to us, or credited to our account. Although we will still struggle with sin and frequent failures, God has legally declared us to be right with Him, and He treats us that way (Romans 8:33–34; 2 Corinthians 5:21).

Third, the Christian has been adopted. God is the Creator, sovereign, and judge of all humanity. To us who believe, however, He is also our Father (Galatians 4:5; Ephesians 1:5). Through faith in Christ, we have been adopted into God's family and enjoy all the privileges of sonship (John 1:12). Though it may seem too wonderful to be true, God loves us as He loves His own Son (John 17:23) and gives us His Spirit as a pledge of our future inheritance (Romans 8:15; Ephesians 1:13–14).

Fourth, the Christian is indwelt with the Spirit of God. We do not walk through this world alone; Christ has sent the Holy Spirit to dwell within us (John 14:16–17). The Spirit testifies of Christ, teaches, leads, helps, convicts, and serves as a pledge for the fullness of God that awaits the believer in heaven (John 14:16; 15:26; 16:7–8; Romans 8:14; 2 Corinthians 1:22; 5:5; Ephesians 1:14; 1 John 2:27). Through the person of the Holy Spirit, Jesus Christ continues to be our Immanuel, which means "God with us" (Isaiah 7:14; Matthew 1:23).

Fifth, the Christian has been given eternal life. It is important to understand that eternal life began for us the moment we believed in Jesus Christ (John 5:24). Eternal life is more than a quantity of life (life without end); it is also a quality of life (life in fellowship with God). Jesus said, "This is eternal life, that they may know You, the only true God, and Jesus Christ whom You have sent" (John 17:3).

Sixth, the Christian is God's workmanship. One of the greatest evidences that God has justified us is that He continues to sanctify us—that is, He works in our lives to make us holy. The Bible teaches us that God is directing all things in our lives, even His discipline, so that we will be conformed to the image of Christ and do the good works that He prepared beforehand for us to do (Romans 8:28–29; Ephesians 2:10; Hebrews 12:5–11). What a privilege to know that God will be relentless in working for our transformation. The apostle Paul wrote that he was "confident of this very thing, that He who has begun a good work in you will complete it until the day of Jesus Christ" (Philippians 1:6).

Finally, the Christian will be glorified. Our great and certain hope is that because Christ has risen, we also will be raised from the dead and glorified when Christ returns (Romans 8:11, 17, 29–30). Our mortal bodies will be transformed into conformity to Christ's glorious body and will no longer be subject to sin, death, or corruption (1 Corinthians 15:53–54; Philippians 3:20–21; 1 Thessalonians 4:16–17). We will forever be with the Lord in a new heaven and a new earth in which only righteousness dwells (John 14:2; 1 Thessalonians 4:17; 2 Peter 3:13; Revelation 21:1–4, 22–27).

HOW THEN SHALL WE LIVE?

The Bible calls us to live in a manner that is worthy of our calling (Ephesians 4:1), to grow in conformity to the image of Christ (Romans 8:29), and to walk in the good works that God has prepared for us to do (Ephesians 2:10). In response to the mercies of God, we should present our lives to God as living sacrifices, holy and acceptable to Him (Romans 12:1–2). The following practical guidelines are taken from the Bible in order to aid us in this magnificent quest.

STUDY THE BIBLE

We must grow in our knowledge of God, our knowledge of all that He has done for us in Christ, and our knowledge of His will for our lives. We must be strengthened in our faith, encouraged in our obedience, and conformed to the image of God. This can be accomplished only through reading, studying, memorizing, and obeying the Bible. The Bible is inspired by God and is profitable for teaching, rebuking, correction, and training in righteousness (2 Timothy 3:15–17). For this reason, we must be diligent to know its truths and apply them to our lives (2 Timothy 2:15). Jesus said, "Man shall not live by bread alone, but by every word that proceeds from the mouth of God" (Matthew 4:4).

DEVOTION TO PRAYER

God speaks to us through the Bible, and we speak to God through prayer. We can do nothing by ourselves (John 15:4–5), but we can become fruitful by depending on Christ's power and making our needs known to Him in prayer (John 15:7–8). The Bible abounds with teachings on the necessity of prayer, the benefits of prayer, and the promises of blessing for all who pray (Matthew 7:7–11; Luke 11:1–13; James 4:2). For these reasons and more, we should devote ourselves to prayer and never lose heart (Luke 18:1; Colossians 4:2).

Prayer is communing and conversing with God. It includes worship, or praise; giving thanks; requesting that God's will might be accomplished in our lives, our families, our churches, and the world; requesting that God would meet our needs according to His wisdom; and confessing sin and requesting spiritual strength to overcome. One of the best ways to learn to pray is to study the prayers of the Bible. One of the most helpful is the model prayer found in Matthew 6:9–13.

PUBLIC IDENTIFICATION WITH CHRIST THROUGH BAPTISM

We are saved by faith alone, but Christ commands those who believe to publicly identify with Him and His people through baptism (Matthew 28:18–20; Acts 8:36–37).

FELLOWSHIP WITH A BIBLICAL CHURCH

It is God's will that all true believers unite themselves with a community of like-minded believers (Hebrews 10:23–25). Some of the characteristics of a biblical church include the following:

- a commitment to the inerrancy and sufficiency of the Bible
- an appreciation for biblical truth and a passion to preach and teach it
- a fidelity to orthodox, Trinitarian Christianity, such as is found in the classic confessions of faith arising from the Reformation
- a high view of God and a recognition of man's sinfulness and need
- the conviction that Christ and His gospel are central and preeminent in the Christian faith
- a biblical understanding of conversion leading to repentance, faith, and holiness
- a dedication to biblical worship in the fear of God in contrast to entertainment or emotionalism
- leadership consisting of men who are holy, humble, and able to teach, who lay down their lives for the believers under their care and exercise pastoral discipline over them
- a commitment to biblical counseling and church discipline
- a genuine pursuit of Christlikeness, holiness, and love with a brokenness over its own shortcomings and a refusal to exalt itself over other sound and faithful churches
- a real and observable commitment to evangelism and missions
- a dependence upon God expressed in regular meetings for fervent prayer

GROWTH IN SANCTIFICATION

The Bible teaches us that sanctification (our personal growth in holiness, or Christlikeness) is the will of God (1 Thessalonians 4:3; Hebrews 12:14; 1 Peter 1:14–16). For this to become a reality in our lives, we must pursue God through reading the Bible, prayer, fellowship with godly believers, and abstaining from the sinful things of this world lest they contaminate us (2 Corinthians 6:14–7:1).

SERVICE IN THE LOCAL CHURCH

The Bible teaches us that every believer is part of a royal priesthood (1 Peter 2:9). Each of us has been given spiritual gifts (abilities) that are to be used for the building up of the local church (Romans 12:4–8; 1 Corinthians 12:4–7). We should not merely join a biblical church; we must serve in the church according to our abilities. The ministry in the church is not confined to the pastors or elders. The pastors are to equip all the members in the church for the work of the ministry (Ephesians 4:11–12).

SERVICE IN EVANGELISM AND MISSIONS

It is the will of God that the gospel of Jesus Christ be preached to all nations and to every person under heaven (Mark 16:15; Luke 24:47). Christ's command has been called the Great Commission (Matthew 28:18–20), and each Christian is to be committed to this task according to his or her gifts. This also includes caring for Christians who are persecuted for the faith, helping those who suffer need, and doing works of charity for those who do not believe (Matthew 25:31–46; Galatians 6:10; Hebrews 13:3, 16; James 1:27).

OUR HOPE AND PRAYER FOR YOU

Now may the God of peace Himself sanctify you completely; and may your whole spirit, soul, and body be preserved blameless at the coming of our Lord Jesus Christ.

—1 Thessalonians 5:23